Well-being for Children

Yukari Takata

For children of Injambakkam school

I wish to teach the children of Injambakkam school about health education programs. With the help of this book, children would be able to learn about ways to become healthy. They will learn about their physical health, mental health, and the social impacts in their life. It could prevent and avoid many problems, and dangerous things happening around their life.

Contents

Social health

14. Group play with friends.

15. The world is made of diversity.

16. Stop bullying.

17. Learn to protect babies.

18. Problems of child labor.

19. Keep surrounding areas clean.

Avoidance of problems and knowledge of security

20. Have the right judgement and act promptly.

21. Every second counts for cooling the burn!

22. Be careful of the sea and the river.

23. Be careful of the load.

24. My body is mine.

Physical health

1. Why do you need to be clean?

 You cannot see germs with your eyes, but there are germs around you. Cleanliness prevents you from getting sick. You need to wash your hands, wash your hair and body, wash your clothes, and keep your room clean. A clean appearance makes a good impression about you.

How to adopt cleanliness!

Good impression!!

Wash your palm and the back of the hand.

Wash between fingers and each finger one by the one.

If you wash your hands for 30 seconds, you decrease 1/100 of germs !

Wash and turn your nails. Don't forget to wash your wrist!

 Try to clean up your room every day. It feels better to be in a clean and pleasant room! So, you need to get fresh air in your room. If you are in a small room, you can circulate the air by opening the window for a short time every day. Sunrise is good to suppress germs. On a sunny day, you may try to dry the carpet and cushions outside. Sanitization is also possible in boiling water. But, you should be careful not to burn yourself. You need the help of an adult!

2. What kind of food do you eat?
 We cannot live if we do not eat properly. If you eat many sweet candies and fried snacks, you cannot have a strong healthy body. Human body needs many nutrients. It is important to take a good balanced food. As much as possible, you should choose fresh vegetables, fruits, and good ingredients to eat.

 Water is very important for our bodies. If water is lost from the human body, you cannot be healthy. In particular, you must not forget to drink water whenever there is high temperature and humidity. Even if you stay inside, you should be careful to hydrate yourself. Hydration makes your body cooler.

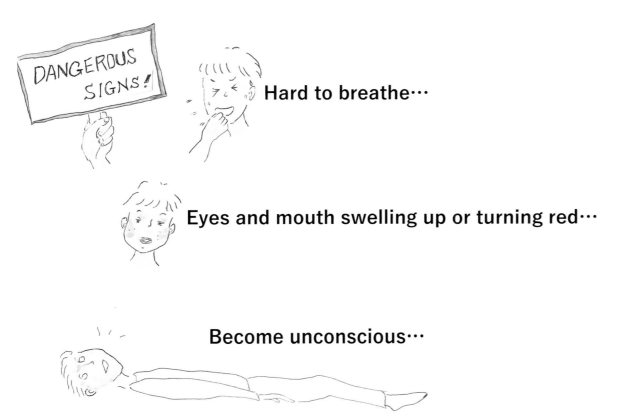

Hard to breathe…

Eyes and mouth swelling up or turning red…

Become unconscious…

Typical food allergies

… Peanuts

… Milk

… Egg

… Sea food

… Wheat

… Nuts

 If a person has an allergy for a particular type of food, it can cause panic and even death. Typical food allergies are peanuts, nuts(cashew nut, walnut), wheat, egg, milk, and sea foods. If you find immediate symptoms, like your mouth getting rashes, your eyes and face swelling up, your skin turning red or breathing becoming difficult, it is very dangerous! You should immediately call and tell an adult. You must also keep calm and wait for an ambulance.

3. You need to go to the toilet.

How many times do you go to the toilet? Usually, people go to the toilet 5~6 times a day. If you go to the toilet only a few times a day or hold it back, it is not good for your body. When germs increase in your bladder, you will fall sick and pain will occur during urine flows.

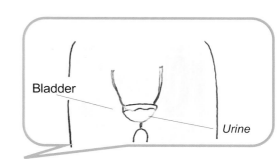

Bladder is a bag which holds urine.

You must change your underwear every day. Girls and babies are easily infected from the part where urine flows. If your underwear falls to the ground, you need to wash it again. Wet underwear easily increases germs. As much as possible, dry it in the sun.

Do you have regular motion? If you don't have motion once in 1-2 days, it's called constipation. You should tell your parents. You will have to check if you are eating fiber foods. For example, banana or cabbage.

Stool : *If it is too hard or watery, you need to take enough water. Check what you ate last night and today. It is important to check your body regularly.*

Which type was it today?!

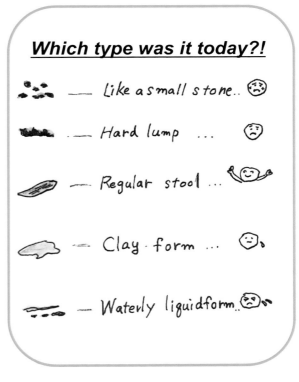

Urine: *Normally, the urine that just flows out is germfree. If it is muddy, your urine is infected by germs.*

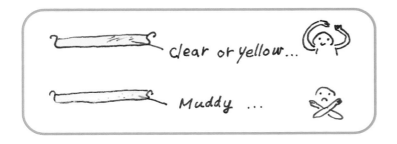

Check your urine and stool regularly!

4. Caring for your head and eyes.

If you fall down from a high place and hit your head, it is a dangerous situation. After having hit the head, do you think it is safe that you did not cry or did not bleed? It is not a right judgment. If consciousness does not become clear and vomiting occurs, you must go to the hospital immediately (as an emergency case).

Within 48 hours of hitting your head, in other words, next 2 days, if you vomit suddenly, you must go to hospital as soon as possible. In this case, vomiting is not due to stomach becoming upset. It is possibly due to the damage in the brain.

Delicate eyes

 As for the eyes, a part of the brain is stretched in a process of evolution. So, eyes are very delicate. If something hits in your eye and you've had an injury, if you cannot open your eyes, it is a serious case! You must hurry, and you have it examined by a doctor.

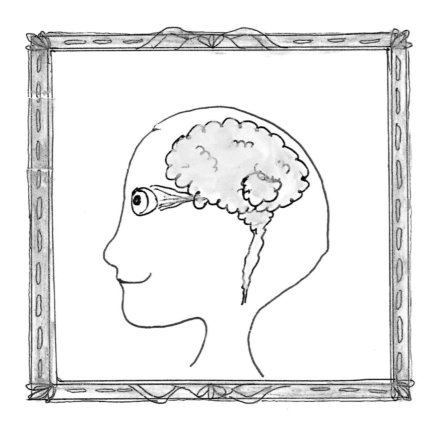

 When you study or read a book, you must be careful to ensure that your table and book has enough light.

5. Importance of brushing your teeth.

 Do you brush your teeth in the morning and before sleep at night? If you have nice clean teeth and no cavities, it is as valuable as having a property in your life. Cavity is a sickness and an infection, and if the cavity continues to get worse, you must go to a dentist. If you do not treat your cavity, your tooth will start to hurt, and begin to decay.

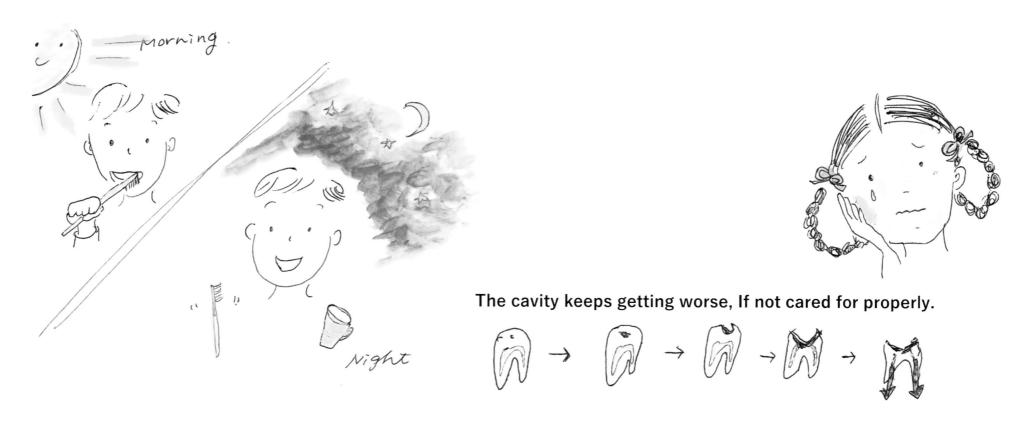

The cavity keeps getting worse, If not cared for properly.

The tooth that decays has a hole. Germs invades your body through the tooth hole. It is very dangerous. It is better to treat the problem of your milk teeth to ensure that you will not have problem for the permanent teeth. Otherwise, when you become an adult, it might cost you a lot. You should brush your teeth to protect yourself from cavities every day.

6. Keeping your nose and ears clean.

Do you keep your nose clean? When there is a cold going around, you must wash your nose and hands when you return home. The wet cavity of our nose and small hair of nose prevents entry of germs through moisture. However, if we breathe through our mouth, it cannot filter germs.

What's the color?!

Keep your nose clean and blow your nose!

Small hairs

When your mucus flows, you need check your mucus, it's color, and how many days you've been having mucus. The normal mucus is clear in color, but greenish or yellow mucus has germs! If you have greenish or yellow mucus for 3 days, you should go to the doctor. If you keep on continuing to have dirty mucus, you will start to have a headache, bad smell in your nose, and lose your concentration.

In the evening, if the doctor's clinic is closed, and you suddenly have a pain in the ear, you must not wait until the next morning. You have to tell your parents. Even if the doctor is closed for the day, you can ask for medicine at the pharmacy.

You should never shout loudly near the ear of your friend !

7. Relationship between sleep and light.

Sleep will help you recover from being tired. Your good night's sleep has a relationship with your growing up and in controlling your skin as well. Sleep is related to mental health. Even a gentle person becomes very annoyed due to lack of sleep. When you see the morning sun, you wake up, flash and you are happy. Human eyes recognize light and send information to the brain that it is time to 'Wake up!' The brain controls the rhythm of the day.

For you to sleep well and wake up energetic in the morning, you need to get morning sunlight every day. At night, stay away from bright light. It is not good that you watch television or use the cell-phone for a long time, or if your room is too bright before you go to bed. To have a sound sleep, you should stay away from bright light before sleeping.

Before you sleep...

8. Importance of Exercise and Martial arts.

 Do you always play with friends happily, and with full of vitality? Not only does exercise let your body grow, it also lets you feel bright and cheerful. It is nice to play outside with friends. It is not a problem if you do not like to exercise regularly. But it is important that you do exercise a few times a week. You can do exercises and dance without spending money.

I recommend you to learn martial arts. Martial arts not only builds up your body, but it even helps to defend yourself. You can learn good manners and personal relationships from the martial arts with your teacher and friends of different ages.

Karate is not only to fight for strength, it has a beauty of its own. If you learn well, your appearance, concentration will increase. Of course, your mental health will also improve.

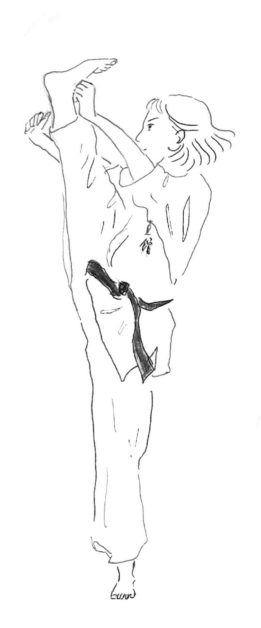

Mental health

9. A disease of mind.

In mental health problems even if a person does not have a sickness, it cannot be said that he is happy and healthy. There are many kinds of mental illness. There is "depression". Depression is a feeling of sadness and loss of energy during the day, it is difficult to cope with normal routine.

Depression can affect anyone. Even a cheerful person can get this sickness. And many a times, the person does not notice it himself. It is not easy to treat this sickness alone, even your family or best friend may not be able to help. So, the help of other people is necessary, and you need to see a doctor.

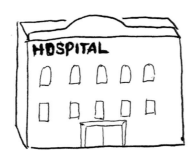

10. Addiction to alcohol.

Children must not drink alcohol because it interferes with their growth. The one dangerous side of alcohol is that one cannot stop drinking it once it becomes a habit. When one cannot control drinking alcohol, it affects his family, friends, and work.

Addiction to alcohol changes the person's gentle nature so much, that he will betray his family and drink alcohol. Because this is also a sickness, he has to go to the hospital and be treated by doctors before it is too late.

11. Smoking is injurious to health.

In the world, there are so many people who cannot stop smoking. It is not easy to stop smoking, no matter how strong-willed a person is. Because smoking is a disease, it is called the nicotine dependency. This disease is very strong in dependence. Do NOT be one among them.

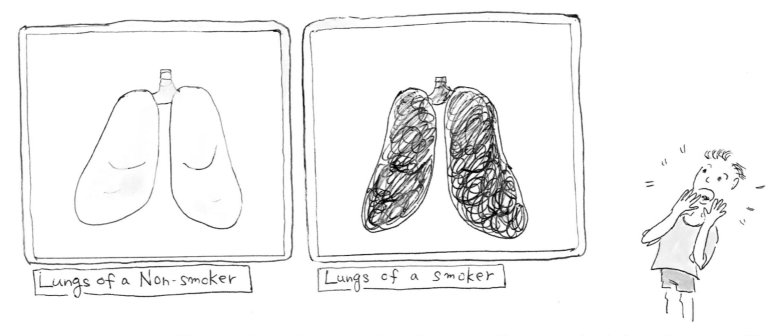

Lungs of a Non-smoker

Lungs of a Smoker

Non-smoker's lung is pink and healthy. But a smoker's lung is smutty like coal-tar.

Further, for smoking you need to spend lots of money. There are also medical expenses. How much do you think are the costs of a cigarettes for one month and one year? Smoking also causes cancer of mouth, throat, and lungs. You can spend money on more important things in life.

 1 box for 1 day.

 7 boxes for 1 week.

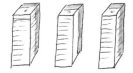 **30 boxes for 1 month.**

365 boxes for 1 year.
How much does it cost you?!
A lot of money!!!

12. Never use narcotic drugs.

Drugs must not be even be tried once. Even if you are invited by your friend, you must have the courage to refuse. When humans and animals use drugs, their brain and their thinking changes. Once the brain is changed by drugs, even a strong-willed person cannot refuse drugs.

Therefore, drugs are prohibited by the law. Taking drugs is a crime. Drugs destroy your health, your mind, your family, your happiness and ultimately takes away your life.

You should have courage to say NO ! !

"This is fun! Would you like to try it?"
➡ **You had better know that taking drugs is a crime.**

Even if they say "It is legal!"
➡ **It is illegal to use it. The legal drugs that are available are usable only during hospital admission.**

"If you decline drugs, I will not let you join me!"
➡ **Are these words that your friend said? If your friend has said those words, then he is NOT your true friend.**

13. Laughter is good for health.

Do you laugh at least once in a day? As for laughing, it is important for refreshment and relaxation. It is good to laugh, for your health's sake, because its affects emotion, and changes the atmosphere around you. Furthermore, laughter spreads from person to person.

As for your smile, let it go around and make the people near you also smile. If you are happy, you make others happy too. Let us take in laughter every day as a healthy medicine in our lives.

If you are not smiling...   *No one else smiles.*

If you are smiling...   *Everyone smiles!!*

Social health

14. Group play with friends.

 When you play tag with your friends, you include physical exercise which is important for your growth. There are many movements, that you can try out. For example, to run, to chase after, and to catch. In this way, you learn to get along with other friends, you also get good exercise of balancing. It is much better than playing alone.

Further, children get to learn the social value of experience from group play with friends. In a group play with friends, there is a leader of the group and each play a different role. This group playing is just a scaled-down version in society. Through this playing, one learns. They learn human relations and leadership qualities before becoming adults.

To the adult society...

15. The world is made of diversity.

 There are people who are born with disability, and people who become disabled by accident or sickness. Anyone may become disabled, or you may have a child with a disability. If such is the case, and no one comes to help you and your family, you will be so sad, isn't it?

 In this world, there are different types of people with, various religions and races. From youngsters to the elderly, sick persons to healthy people. Naturally, it includes persons with disabilities too.

May I help you?

Thank you.

Human society is made up of diversity. If their inconvenience is helped by everybody, this world will become more comfortable and a happier place live in.

Look at picture above. It looks a boy, but the heart is that of a girl. Or it looks a girl, but the heart is that of a boy. Even if the sex of the heart is different around us. It is not wrong. It is not strange!

16. Stop bullying.

Bullying is not only a physical violence like a kick. Bullying includes mental violence. For example, the violence of words, or hurting of feelings. If you are being bullied, you must ask for help from an adult. You are not bad, the person who does the bullying is the bad person.

If you are just looking at it from a distance, it is the same as if you are accepting the bullying process.

An onlooker of bullying

Bullying

Victim

Did you notice bullying around you? If you are just looking at it, it is the same as if you accept this bullying*. You must not be an onlooker of the bullying. You must complain to the teacher. Let us take action to stop bullying.

* Yohji Morita: Four-layer structure model of ijime; International Journal of Bullying Prevention(2020)2:324-325

17. Learn to protect babies.

Let us all guard babies. Babies are gifts to our society. To protect and save the baby, it is necessary for you to know the nature of the baby. You should understand that a sleeping baby may roll-over suddenly. Do not put the baby on a table or at an elevated position. Never leave the baby alone near a water body. You must keep the baby away from electric cords and plug sockets. The baby's nature is to take everything to its mouth. You must keep away things smaller than the baby's mouth away from the baby.

33mm

Things less than this size are dangerous!

Be careful! Baby signs of dehydration

He/she is not in good spirits, or He/she is in a bad mood

Top of the head sinks.
His/her lips are dry.
Less volume of urine, or no urine and no tears.

Babies and infants get dehydrated more easily than adults.

18. Child labor.

Child labor is when children are stopped from going school. It interrupts their health. It is dangerous to harm, or exploit a child. For example, unfair wages or labor is also a crime. Child work is helping only his/her house or working for their future. If the child's work is very hard in their house too and the child cannot go to school, it's the same as child labor.

You've heard that the duty of the child is to study at school. Because, at school, you can learn useful things for your future with friends. And it increases the choices of your occupation in future. There is a wonderful system for elimination of child labor (by Akshara foundation*). In this school, older students teach the younger students, and older students earn reward points. These points can be exchanged for essential items, like snacks, shoes, clothes, and toys!

*Akshara foundation: https://akshara.org.in

19. Keep surrounding areas clean.

"The plastic returns to the soil."

No! Plastic remains in the soil, river, and sea!

"Someone will clean up this trash."

No! If you hadn't thrown it away, the cleaner could have cleaned up other places.

"No problem, it is not my house area."

No! If someone throws trash in front of your house, you would not like it.

"Nobody is seeing it. I don't mind it."

No! Even though nobody has seen it, God is seeing your act.

If you keep throwing away small trash everyday for one whole year ?..

Trash..

365 trashes!! Imagine this situation.

Sad...

Where does trash and garbage go?

 The trash thrown away by everyone pollutes our soil, sea, and air. Later it contaminates the food, water and air. It also enters directly or indirectly into our bodies. This is a big problem of the world. We should think about this problem. The first step, we must stop throwing waste everywhere.

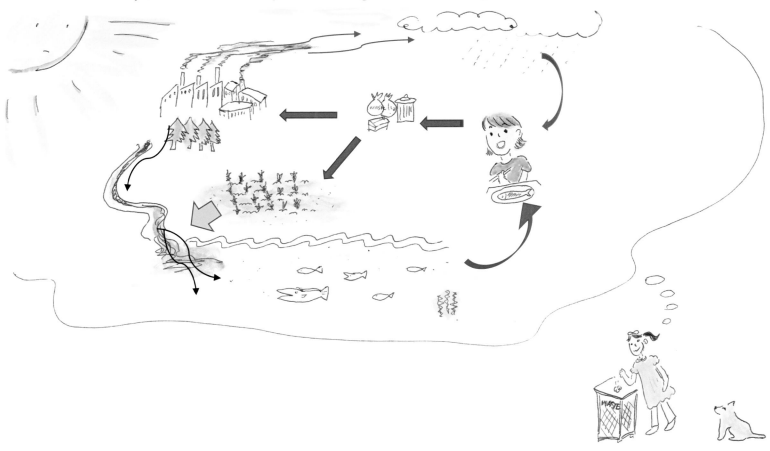

Avoiding problems and knowledge of security

20. Have the right judgement and act promptly.

When a disaster suddenly happens, most people in an accident stand with shock for a while like a 'freeze' as mentioned Dr Leach.* Why is it that in a situation like this the people are 'frozen'? This is due to one of part of the human brain.

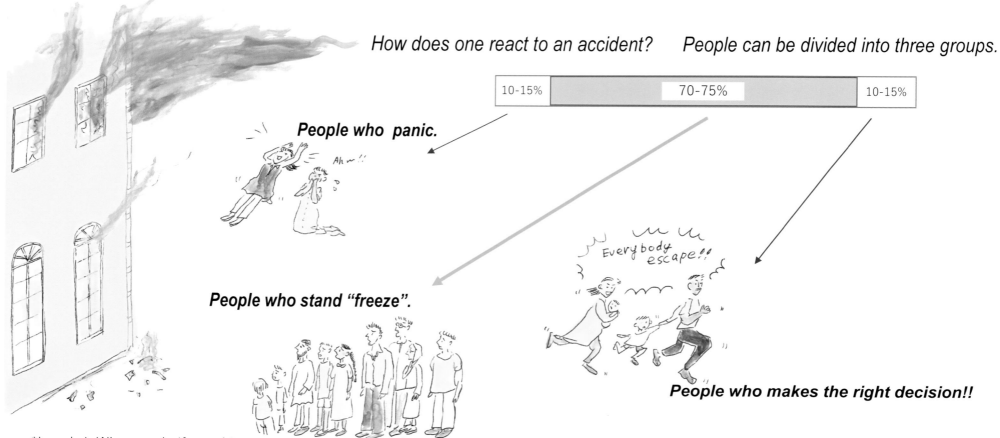

How does one react to an accident?　People can be divided into three groups.

| 10-15% | 70-75% | 10-15% |

People who panic.

People who stand "freeze".

Everybody escape!!

People who makes the right decision!!

*Leach J: Why people 'freeze' in an emergency: temporal and cognitive constraints on survival responses. Aviat Space Environ Med 2004;75:539-542

What should we do to prevent 'freeze'? If you encounter disaster, you have to change the state of your 'freeze' and panic due to fear and shock. You should have the right judgement and act promptly. And it always helps you to practice a disaster prevention drill.

Smoke is dangerous too. You cannot run away when you have inhaled toxic smoke for even a few minutes. You must escape by lowering yourself. And you must cover your mouth with cloth. Find a way to escape by keeping very close to the wall.

How would I be able to escape if a fire happens in my house or school?

21. Every second counts for cooling the burn!

You must cool the burn with water, and earlier the better, Do not wait even for 1 second! The burn soaks quickly into the skin. If you have spilled boiled water on your clothes, you do not have time to take off the clothes. It is an emergency! The first aid that you must do is to cool the burn with a lot of cold water.

You don't have time to take off the clothes!!

56

Human skin is made of 3 levels. You must hurry to stop a burn at the surface of the skin of level 1. The burn does not absorb heat into skin too much. Remember to keep hot water away from an infant.

Human skin

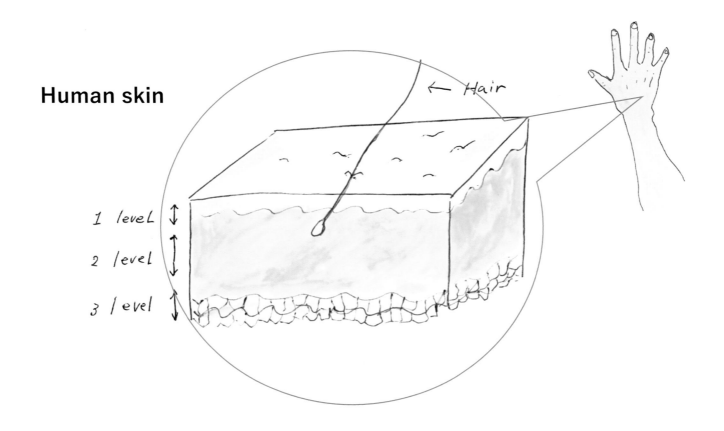

← Hair

1 level ↕
2 level ↕
3 level ↕

22. Be careful of the sea and the river.

 While on a beach, the wave can suddenly withdraw away from the shore into the sea. This wave is called rip current. Rip currents can carry away even the strongest swimmer toward the sea and he/she may not be able to come back to the shore. Furthermore, as for this wave, it cannot be visually seen from beach.

This is a rip current.

Help!!

In a river after it has rained, the water level will rise within a few minutes. You must not approach near the river even if rains have stopped. Don't go into water when there is a flood. If water comes above your knee, it is in danger level. You would not be able to control yourself if the water is above the knee.

When there is flood, the manhole hatch may float. You must not pass over manholes, sewage and drains. If the sea or nearby river overflows, You must seriously consider how you can escape to a safer place.

If there is water above your knees, danger is HIGH!

The manhole hatch may float in case of excessive flooding.

23. Be careful of the road.

When you cross the road, look to the right, to the left, and once again to the right!
In the shaded part of this figure, the driver cannot see the height of the child from the driver's seat of the car. Particularly, it is dangerous when you walk along the backside of a parked car. When the car moves, the car might go back suddenly.

Shaded part

Don't play!

Don't play in the car parking lot!

There can be serious injuries to the head in case of an accident by motorcycle or bicycle. The injury may strongly strike on the head. It is similar to a block having fallen on your head.
If you put on a helmet, it will protect your head and life.

You should put on a helmet when you ride a bicycle or motorcycle!

24. My body is mine.
 There is a person aiming at a child everywhere. A person aiming at a child may sometimes be someone whom you know. Even if you are a boy, you must be careful in the same way as a girl. You must not allow anyone to see and touch your private part or your underwear.
 It is only you who own your body. It should only be your mother or your doctor when you are sick who can see and touch you.

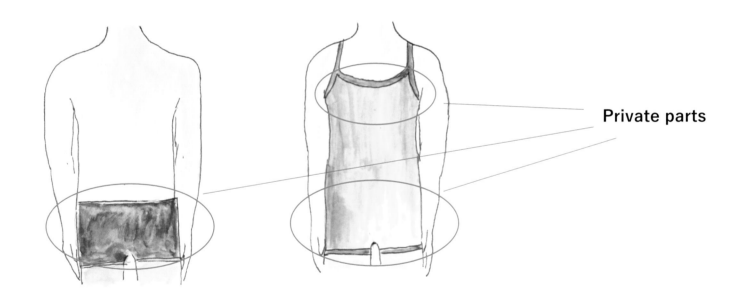

Private parts

Do not take nude photographs of yourself and send to others. No one should touch your private parts. In case they do so, you have to escape from them and tell your mother, your teacher or a reliable person. You should not be ashamed. The person is wrong,
you are not wrong about anything.

Well-being for children

2023 年 7 月 11 日 初版発行

著　者　高田　由香理

定　価　本体価格 3,000 円+税

発行所　株式会社　三恵社
　　　　〒462-0056 愛知県名古屋市北区中丸町 2-24-1
　　　　TEL 052-915-5211　FAX 052-915-5019
　　　　URL http://www.sankeisha.com

ISBN978-4-86693-827-1　C8737

Author introduction : Yukari Takata

Born in Kobe Japan in 1972 she secured her Masters degree in Early Childhood Education from Hyogo University of Teacher Education.

She is engaged in nursing duties at the Department of Gynecology and Pediatrics. She has given lectures in various topics including the health education of children and special kids needs care as part of nursery teacher training in junior college.